GENEALOGY RESEARCH
How to Organize the Notes, Papers, Documents, Emails, Scans, Computer Files, and Photographs for Family Research

D. Kalten

Revised Jan 2015

.

This is the black and white visual version of *How to Organize Genealogy Research.*

.

GENEALOGY RESEARCH
How to Organize the Notes, Papers, Documents, Emails,
Scans, Computer Files, and Photographs for Family Research

Visuals are shown in black and white.

Dedication

This work is dedicated to YOU, the person who would like to preserve the existence and history of family members.

You are the person who is willing to take the time to put things down to pass on to future family members and share with those now living. You deserve credit for your time and efforts.

*

Table of Contents

*

Introduction

This book is designed as an easy read to get you organized with all of your notes, papers, documents, family stories, photographs and other items that you have and as always happens, are still searching for. It also advises on what to do after you are organized with some tips.

You may have found that a lot of information for your early family members can be found on the web and that adds to your collection of treasures found with it is turning into a confusing mess.

The thought of 'what should you do to keep organized' may be running thru your mind and you are probably overwhelmed with feeling very disorganized. Many who have been doing genealogy research (family research) for a long time has or has had an organization problem and are tired of all the assorted confusions and clutter, both with paper and within their computer. There are usually a lot of photographs to organize and do something with also.

What can you do? The answers are within this book, sometimes with options, as each has their own personal preferences. Following these pages is your easy way to organization. You may find that you have things you forgot about, or information you did not realize you actually had.

You will find tips on what not to do within this book and those are wise to follow to avoid added work and time.

Organization will help eliminate errors and that organization may show you some missing facts.

There are free programs listed on some pages to help you. I have no connection to any of them.

*

Forward: Simply Put ......

Do NOT work when you are tired.

- It is too easy to do errors.

- It is too easy to try to take shortcuts.

- It is too easy to totally confuse yourself and miss steps or forget something.

- It is too easy to attach a person to the wrong person and suddenly realize one day that you have (example) your child as your parent or a grandchild of your own listed as a sibling to one of your parents.

ROUTINE:

- This book gives you the basics of what you need to do and puts it in a format to follow. If you choose to change your own routine, that is fine.

- Do NOT miss any steps.

- Make yourself a 'Routine List' that works for you after you understand everything within these pages.

Your OVERALL Goals:

- Organize and file all paper documents.

- Make and Organize genealogy computer files.

- Scan all original documents.

- Scan Photographs, Bible pages, etc.

- Email organization of old contacts and information.

- Retaining every little fact that there is that you currently have.

- Working with a genealogy program.

*

Chapter 1 – Simple Tools Needed

Trying to get your family paper treasures organized does require a few things, some of which you may already have. Without the proper items it would be like trying to boil water without heat. You will FIRST need to make sure you have these items. I will refer to them as your 'tools' and they are NOT expensive.

It will be assumed that you have a computer, HOWEVER if you do not have a computer just substitute the word 'paper' in place of it where it is applicable throughout these pages.

...

If you do not have a computer, you would be very wise to get one. Some think they have to learn 'THE computer'. NO, you have to learn some basic, very simple computer basics (like how to turn it on, off, free security programs and keystrokes) and the programs you will use. Your goal is to enter information and save it. The advantage of what you can do with a computer will shock you.

Many people think they do not need a computer as they can access what they need by phone or whatever new electronic gismo comes on the market. This is wrong! Can you picture a large department store keeping track of all their inventory purchases, current inventory, items sold, store sales, refunds and payroll without a computer? It would be massive paper work without one.

...

What You Need – Your Supply List

1: Get at least one CLEAR plastic file tub to start.

These are the stackable type with lids and are available in any office supply or large multi-product store. Try to keep your lid color clear, white or black so that they are a neutral color and if you need to buy more, you can hopefully match them. Watch for a good sale and that does happen often. If funds allow, get what you think you will need keeping in mind the future things you hope to find or order, NOT things found on the web. If you are not using a computer, you will need many more than a person using a computer. How many tubs you will need depends on what you have, what you hope to find and if you will be following every line for both male and female family members. REMEMBER, if you are using a computer, these are for original documents, not scanned or web found items.

DO get at least one extra to hold books that may have family mentioned and possible other items that are too large to 'file'.

Do NOT get a large metal or wood two or four drawer file cabinet as they are heavy to move, are much heavier when full, are bulky, do rust, can get damaged, are hard to conceal and are not waterproof. The plastic file containers can be stacked or layered in a closet, a basement, an attic or in your work room when you are done with them. You want your work to survive past you so think of the ease of moving and storing the plastic ones vs metal or wood file cabinets. If you are limited on space, stacking two or two stacks of two and putting a table cloth over them can actually become an end table, an end table that can be a 'show and tell'.

Another advantage with using the plastic tubs is that they can easily be replaced if for some reason one may crack. If you have the wood or metal file cabinets, years of dings, scratches and other abuse can lead to drawers not working correctly and an overall ugly appearance. You also cannot easily hide the wood or metal cabinets so they are there to see in whatever room you place them. As far as damage, when you wash the floor or the carpeting, that starts the damage to the metal with rust or with wood, warping and discoloring at the bottom.

2: File Jackets:

These are the manila colored file folders that all offices use. Get the standard size, not legal size. Legal size will not be needed often, if at all, and you do want the folders to fit in your file containers and filed, not lying in the bottom under regular sized folders. For legal size papers, you will have to fold them.

DO get the STRAIGHT EDGE, open side file folders. The divided tab folders will not mean a thing when you start adding in more people alphabetically. The straight edge also gives you enough writing room. You want the standard ones, not ones that expand. Over time, you can always invest in expandable ones if needed for a person and remember they come in varied expandable sizes. The expandable ones are closed sides. Should you need more than one folder for one person and do not have any expandable folders, you can do 'Folder 1 of X' in pencil on the far right of the label.

Do NOT get the colored file folders thinking that you are going to color code family lines. It does not work. Each generation doubles people and ads in new surnames considering the female lines. By the time you get to just a few generations back you will be out of color options to buy. Also, further down the lineage you easily have to have multi-colors for each person. Do not drive yourself crazy with expensive color file jackets or try any other color coding with paper files. You can rely on name and dates for your files. Your genealogy program will come into play with keeping track of family lines. The goal with these folders is paper organizing, not family line sorting.

3: Mechanical Pencils.

Mechanical pencils come in varied brands but the cheap ones can be very hard to read due to the nature of the pencil lead they use. Look for Paper-Mate Sharp Writer #2 USA which come in a deep yellow. They are not expensive. I have seen them at all office supply stores and dollar classed type stores.

Keep one near you and remember that a pen can be your worst enemy.

4: Sharpies.

You want at least one Extra Fine and one wide black Sharpie permanent ink pen.

5: Yellow self-stick papers often called 'stickies' and sticky note sheets.

Get some yellow self-stick paper tablets. There are varied brands at a variety of prices. A size around 2" to 3" or 2" x 4" square is usually sufficient. This may be needed to add a note onto a paper original or whatever little need you may run across.

6: Genealogy Computer Program.

You should have a computer and a computer program in this modern day. It will greatly open up what you can do, what you can find and will keep your information quickly down in a readable sense for your family connections.

7: Computer program Word or equivalent.

You will need the Microsoft program known as Word Document or an equal to it. If you do not have Word Document, see the free program at www.openoffice.org/product/writer.html as you will have many uses for this type of program.

8: Back Ups.

If you are using a computer, you should have an external drive, thumb drives or some other means of doing backups. You DO want to be able to do backups for your genealogy work, that including photographs and documents you will hold in your computer.

If you choose to pay for an on-line back-up service, that is your choice. However, also do back-ups that you can physically get to.

A free and easy program to download is Karen's Replicator (free with donations welcome). You can set it to backup just your genealogy work and whatever else you chose. You can set it to automatically back up your entire computer or whatever parts you want. An advantage to this program is that you can open your backup and it is just like looking at your computer file folder. You can open a file there and copy from it which is an advantage. It makes it very easy to carry your 'genealogy folder' with you on a thumb drive to view or share (copy and paste) so think of this program for dual   use.
http://www.karenware.com/powertools/ptreplicator.asp

HOWEVER, concerning the above mentioned program, with newer computers it is possible to copy a main folder and 'paste' it to an external drive, a thumb drive or make a copy and transfer it to a CD or CDs. Should you do that, be sure to rename it to identify what it is and when it was done.

9: Optional.

This is an option for special original documents such as a very old original birth certificate that has been handed down to you or one you had to pay big bucks for at a county health department. You may want to find clear plastic sleeves in ARCHIVAL quality for those very special things. There are a variety of brands and they can be found in various office supply stores and outlets. Most tend to be made for ring notebooks but you can find them without that feature which you can use as is or cut the excess off. These will be filed in the above noted manila folders. It IS a good idea to have at least one box of these at hand. The size holds up to 8 1/2" x 11" papers.

For larger paper items you can get large hard plastic holders at some hobby type shops, possibly by special order for specific sizes, and those can be filed in a tub for oversized items. I have purchased those for very old maps in varied sizes.

10: Paper.

Get a pad of paper with lines on it. Not loose paper, but a pad. This is for running notes of things you will think of that you want to do. You will find yourself filing a paper away or maybe doing dishes when you think of something you want to do or need to do concerning research for someone. WRITE it down. You will have a running list, not a page for each thought or person. This is for use even after you are organized. Cross things off as an item is done.

11: The last thing you will need is time, patience and a routine.

Time to work on your organization and the patience to do it is a big key to getting organized. A routine will keep you organized. Never put off a step with what you are doing in the organization category if you want to stay organized. This IS very important.

It is impossible to get organized overnight. It will take some time, that time depending on how many paper and photo treasures you have accumulated. Set your mind that you are going to start at one spot and not deviate from it, even if you can only work a few hours a week on it.

If you have an area of the house where you can leave things out after working on it for a while do so. It helps you stay organized with what you are doing and will allow you to slip in an hour or so of work when you have extra time. It's really hard to organize things when you have to keep gathering things up and hide them. Adding some caution here: If you have pets, try to keep them out of that area when you are not there. Cats love to lay on what you are doing and manage to scatter things.

To sum up this 'tools' section, your first steps, here are your first priorities:

Go shopping and get what you need from the above list.

Figure out what area of the house you are going to work in. Clear out any clutter there and get it ready for you to work in.

Gather your paper documents and various paper treasures.

Set up your TV and/or radio along with possibly a side table for your pop or coffee.

DO finish reading these pages if you have not done so.

*

10

Chapter 2 – Where to Begin with all the Papers

OK, you do have your supplies and are ready to start organizing all of your paper documents.

Keep in mind that this is for only paper documents you have in your possession that are originals. This is NOT for documents you can find on the web or for documents emailed to you unless you have a reason for wanting a paper printed copy. If you do not have a computer, you will be filing all that you do have in these folders.

This is not for coloring coding family lines or for anything else except for filing away in an organized manner original documents. You are currently getting yourself organized to do 'the work' later. More on this is on later pages.

...

First: You are going to start with just one plastic file tub. If you have bought more than one tub, put the others out of the way until you need another. Get that part of the clutter out of your way or you can use them to help divide papers if you chose to do some sorting first. Presorting is not necessary unless you want to see what you have. That is your choice.

Second: Grab two (or four) pieces of printer or copy paper and that WIDE black Sharpie pen. On each paper mark it in BIG lettering 'ORIGINALS – Do NOT Destroy' 'Genealogy Documents' 'A – Z' doing so in three lines and without the quote marks. The first line you may want to underline in red, possibly even using a yellow highlight marker thru those words may be a good idea. Set something of no value under the paper when you do the writing as the ink may bleed through. You are referencing the surname only with the letter the surname begins with.

Put each paper into a clear vinyl paper holder (on the tool list under 'Optional') and tape it with the words facing outwards on at least one side and end on the INSIDE of the tub. This keeps your tub labels from being bent, torn and from getting dirty as files are entered, removed, refiled and tub movements. Use two pieces of scotch tape or clear packaging tape at the top of each to hold each in place.

As you add a file tub for more paper items, change your paper labeling to fit the holdings. The first file tub may soon be 'Genealogy Documents A-N'. Change your labels as you add file tubs with holdings.

Over time as you fill your tub/s you can add paper or thin cardboard dividers between each first letter of files such as between names that begin with A and those that begin with B, labeling each with A or B, and so on. Should you eventually have many tubs and they may contain many surnames beginning with S. You can do dividers between those 'S' names and also note the variations on your tub labels such as SA - SM and SO - SZ.

If you have a tub where the folders you are entering are falling down, which will happen when you begin a tub, add a small empty box to the back of each until it is not needed any further. That also adds a nice place to hold your pens, pencils, yellow sticky paper pads and more.

Third: Get your first blank manila file folder and grab a document. The first paper on the top of the stack is fine. You are going to do folders for people, not for each document!

With your THIN tip black Sharpie pen you are going to label the manila folder. You want the last name, first name, year of birth, and year of death on it starting at the far left. Your folder label will read (example) SMITH Susannah 1875-1952 with no period, no quotes, and no other excess markings.

You can add a note following that IN PENCIL now or later. Leave space between your main label and your added note. Three examples of a full folder heading with a pencil note follow.

Example 1:   SMITH Susannah 1875-1952   Daughter to SMITH John & JONES Mary

Example 2:   SMITH Susannah 1875-1952   3 Marriages: BROWN – SMITH – BING

Example 3:   SMITH Susannah 1875-1952   Maryland research

Again, you are NOT doing folders per document. You are doing folders per person. ALL documents for that person will go into that file folder. Remember you are currently just organizing, NOT doing research. It is very easy to get side tracked. For now, make a note on your pad of paper if you have a thought about doing something concerning someone.

If more than one person is on a document, label and file it under the MAIN person. You can do multi copies in your computer but more on that later. If this is a paper with multi-names, choose the eldest man if he is a main feature on it.

NOTE: Females are listed and filed under their BIRTH name for manila folders and also in a genealogy program. Your pencil note on the right side of the folder tab can be 'Married to XXXX'. Use pencil as label right side notes can easily need changed.

Fourth: Put the folder into your file tub. You have just made and filed your first person folder. Begin with your second folder and person. When or if you come across another document for a person where you have already made a folder, just add the document to it.

Always make sure you do not have a name folder already started for a person with each new document. No matter what type of document you have in your hand, it will go into the person's folder (manila folder) unless it is too large such as a book. In that case, add it to a tub for oversized items and start a list to set in that tub for the contents of it.

Fifth: Continue until you have ALL of your original papers into manila folders and into the file tub/s. If you have a lot of papers and you do not think you will ever get done with folders, keep telling yourself that once they are done you will know what you have and where it is, or another wards, which way is up!

Should you come across a document that you want to add a note to, grab those yellow sticky papers mentioned in 'tools'. Write on the sticky, not on the original. Putting a sticky directly on an original can over time lift the ink off the original so use caution.

If you are entering the document into an archival clear folder first, then write on the BACK side of the yellow sticky. Attach that to the INSIDE front of the plastic holder. The handwriting will face you, will be protected and will not be attached to the original.

When you have all of the papers filed away in your file tub/s, knowing that they are filed in a protected, organized manner for the person they pertain to, you are ready to head to the computer. Your next goal is to scan the original documents but do NOT do so until you read the section concerning the people folders in the computer. Make sure you do not forget that the scans need to be done.

At the point when you have everything into the plastic tubs, you should feel pretty good with your accomplishment!

*

Chapter 3 - Organizing the Computer

All of your original documents that you physically hold should now be filed away in the labeled manila folders and sitting in the plastic file tub/s. Put the lid on them as we will be back to these later as you do have to scan them.

You can do your paper file scans after you understand the folders you have to make, instructions below. This will start the building of people files for EVERYONE you do have any information for. These computer people files will hold EVERYTHING you have for a person, that including things found on the web and even email copies where information pertains to a specific person or people.

You can even begin a file named for a last name only, such as a book or books that mentions many people in a family surname line. Perhaps you have city or county information you want to save. You can begin a folder that says (example) Ohio Montgomery County Dayton city history (no commas).

You DO also want to see the section on photographs. Photographs are the LAST thing to deal with.

This next step in getting organized is to organize all the treasures for your family research that you have in your computer. You are now going to start a file in the computer for each person you have information on within the computer. You will come across things that you may want to check out on the web. DON'T. Later! Make a note on that pad of paper. Remember, you are organizing, not currently doing researching.

FIRST (Folder 1):

You DO need to begin with one main folder that says 'Genealogy Work', (or) 'Family Research', (or) 'Genealogy ALL HERE' or whatever title is comfortable for you (without the quotes). Place that folder on your main desktop screen or in My Documents. You can always drag this main genealogy folder to a different location if you change your mind where you want it. I myself prefer it on my main screen as it is less work for me to find the folder.

If you do not know how to make a folder in your computer follow this: On your main screen you right click, then left click on 'New', and then left click on 'Folder'. Your folder will be yellow in color. The folder titled 'New Folder' will show on your main screen. Go to that folder that says 'New Folder' and it should allow you to change the name. If it does not, do a right click, then a left click on 'Rename'. Enter the folder name.

Your main genealogy folder (level #1)

The goal is to get everything you have concerning your family research into this computer file with subfolders. This includes the original documents you have that should be scanned to the computer. One advantage of having something in your computer is that if you want to check something or pass on a copy, it should be ready to view or pass on to another from these files. Once scanning is done, your original paper items should be filed away in the file tubs and you will have no research reason to get them out. If you want to view an item, open it on your computer where you can enlarge it for viewing if necessary.

Following is how you can file things within your computer to totally stay organized. The goal is that you are going to do people folders, the same as you did for paper documents, only digital.

SECOND (Folder 2):

Begin a subfolder in folder #1, the one you just made. Name it 'People Researched', 'Family Found', 'Family Research – PEOPLE' or whatever name lets you know that each person you have researched or have something for is in this subfolder. I will call this subfolder #2a. As you get familiar with the folders, you can always rename them to suit yourself.

With folder #1 open, do a second subfolder that says 'Genealogy Overflow' which I will call subfolder #2b. This will sit side by side with 'Family Research - People' or whatever name you chose to hold the people.

Family Research - PEOPLE

Genealogy Overflow

Above is folder level #2 showing folder 2a and 2b.

When opening the main genealogy folder, the above is what you should now see (level #2).

The 'Genealogy Overflow' folder will hold varied types of miscellaneous items and you can do subfolders within it for states, maps, links or whatever you need. Let's say you have done a lot of research for Hamilton County in Ohio and have things you want to save for further searches or references. Here you would make a folder saying 'OHIO Hamilton Co' (no quotes). Anything you come across for that county history, maps for it, links for it saved in a Word Document, and other varied miscellaneous items should be placed in that folder if it is something you want to keep.

To give you an example of things to keep, you may find the full city directories on line for a city and you want to keep downloads of the books. You then in the Genealogy Overflow folder make a sub-folder under the state and then under a folder for the county that says City Directories, also naming the place and place them there (example: City Dir Hamilton Co OH).

You can further do other subfolders at deeper levels being levels 2c, 2d, etc. You can add and rearrange whatever you want in 'Genealogy Overflow' other than people. Keep the people in the People folder, folder #2a. Following is a partial view of my 'Genealogy Overflow' which is general information, not information for any direct person. For instance, in the 'Census' folder I have a word document that lists the enumeration dates for all past census years, another for web links and more, all concerning both Federal and State census years, those being divided by two sub-folders to reflect a federal or a state census.

- . Books
- . Cemetery - Headstones
- . CENSUS
- . Countries other than US
- . Deaths
- . FBI The (Genealogy)
- . George Washingtons Journal 1754
- . Google How to Search
- . Illnesses & Diseases
- . Immigration
- . Maps & Links
- . Military & Wars
- . Money Early
- . Names
- . Occupations
- . Photos varied info
- . Quakers

An example of what I have in the federal census folder, the Word document stating the enumeration dates, showing a sentence I have ready for use to copy to a summary is:

1790: The 1st US Federal Census, all information was to reflect the status of each question as of 2 Aug. The family was questioned on XXXX. Note: You fill in the date per family.

Third (folder level # 3) in the PEOPLE FOLDERS:

With the PEOPLE folder open (folder #2a) do a series of folders that say 'A birth names' thru 'Z birth names' without quotes. This will be a folder for every letter of the alphabet. You can make these as you find people or get them all ready now. For less confusion, it is easiest to make them all at once.

A partial view of level #3 with 'U' not added follows:

       Q birth names

       R birth names

       S birth names

       T birth names

       V birth names

       W birth names

Level #3 in the PEOPLE folders

Fourth (folder level #4):

This is sub-folders to the above A to Z sub-folders. AS you begin to add folders for people, first add a folder that says the last name and the words 'birth folder' under the appropriate first letter of the surname. Example: I am one who has SMITH as a research name. So opening the above 'S birth names' folder (level #3), I want to add a folder within it (level #4) that says 'SMITH birth names'. This is where I will find THE PEOPLE BORN who were born as a SMITH.

      SMIT birth name
      SMITH birth name

The previous view shows level #4, a partial view in my 'S birth names' folder.

Fifth (folder level #5):

This IS your people. Here is where you want folders for the individual people. This is within your overall birth name folders.

The files should be named to show last name, first name, then hopefully birth year and the death year. If birth and death are not known, add what best describes a person.

The following example shows a view of my 'SMITH birth name' folder shown in level #4 above. The labels reflect what is best known about each person.

- SMITH Hanna HAMILTON FELIX McKEEVER
- SMITH Isaac ca 1787- born PA
- SMITH Isaac ca 1801-
- SMITH James ca 1800 Ireland-
- SMITH Jane Lacey 1813-1897
- SMITH John W or I.J.orW. ca 1816- born OH
- SMITH Margaret ca 1831- born OH
- SMITH Margaret E ca 1847 - born OH
- SMITH Martha ca 1845- born OH
- SMITH Mary Inez AMONS - GUILD - LUCAS 1834-1907 born OH
- SMITH Mathias ca 1801Germany-
- SMITH Nathaniel ca 1798 NJ-

Above, level 5 is THE people.

Note in the above view of level 5, if I had listed the 'ca' after all of the years, the varied first names for Margaret would show by year of birth in sequence except for the one showing the middle initial.

The goal: You want to file everything for each person under that person's name folder. For example a file named 'SMITH John 1825-1900' should hold everything you have for that John SMITH. If there are eight John Smiths you would have eight folders with each further identified in the folder title as best as you have information for. The birth and death are the best if you know those dates. Note that if you need to use the 'ca' in a date, you need to add it after the year so all years line up in sequence.

SMITH John 1724ca-1724ca bro to John b 1725ca

SMITH John 1725ca-1810ca

SMITH John 1750ca-1848

SMITH John 1775ca-1842

SMITH John 1800ca-1876

SMITH John 1825-1900

SMITH John 1852-1928

SMITH John 1886-1970

Above is another example of level #5 folders.

Try not to get to wordy in your titles as it can interfere with the ability to make further sub-folders under people's names.

To begin with making your first actual person name folder, begin a folder for a name of someone you have in your computer and move whatever may be scattered around in your computer for that person TO that file. The easiest way to do that is to have two windows open, one is for searching and the other one showing the persons folder. Then drag item/s over to it. Just be careful of where you are dragging to and do not work on this if you are tired. It helps to open that person folder and then drag to it.

IF the item you drag to a folder mentions MORE than one person, make a folder for EACH person named in the item. Then go to where the item is, click on 'copy' and then paste a copy into each person folder who was named.

You will most likely have to use your search feature for your computer to find things that you may have.

Do this across the board and get your computer organized. Do not go any further with anything until you have your computer organized with those folder names with all people gathered and put where they belong. If you are holding documents and information on 100 or 10,000 people, for whomever you have a find for, they need a folder even if it is just to hold a Word Document note.

As you get the people folders made, you will see organization building. Do NOT at this time try to organize the contents put into those people folders. You can do that later as you work on a person as explained further in this book. Right now your goal is to get the computer organized and not to be sidetracked from that end of the organization project. Make notes on your pad if need be for a thought on someone or something.

Along the way with building your files, you may want to use the free program (a fast download) that is named CCleaner (https://www.piriform.com/ccleaner) to get rid of a lot of junk like old memory things and various other things that clog up computers. It has various options, one being a cleaner and another being a registry cleaner. IF you are afraid to clean the registry, ignore that part but do use the basic cleaner. It is all mainly old memory things that are cleaned out that you do not want.

You will also have to do 'defrags' now and then since you will be moving a lot of information. Again I stick with the same company and use their free defrag program at https://www.piriform.com/defraggler.

Do not try to put all documents into one mass holding under a document title such as census records. To put it another way, if you have 500 different census records, do not put them all under one file titled census records. You will drive yourself crazy with finding a specific record, if you can remember you have it. Keep everything under a person's name.

For census items, you can do a copy and paste for each person named on a census which in turn helps you build a people file for those people in your computer. The census will give you a 'ca' birth date.

A tip on naming a census find, no matter what family member it is for, title your census label in the following manner, (example) '1930 Census SMITH John HOH 1875-1951' (with no quotes). The 'HOH' means who the head of the household is. The years are his birth and death, if you already know those dates.

If you have a census that has say seven family members noted, copy it to all other six people folders. That copy in each person's folder is ready for when you are ready to research each person and eventually do a final summary for a person, discussed further on other pages.

Folder Level #6:

You may have original old Bible entries, a baptism record, a hand wrote very old letter, military papers, census finds, emails from someone giving you information and a ton of other items for a person. Each should be held in a folder

named as such under that person's NAME FOLDER. You
therefore have a MAIN NAME folder (folder #5 above) with
now a Sixth Level of subfolders, those being the items FOR
an individual person. The following is a small, partial view
of subfolders for a person born as SMITH Mary.

- . 1872 Cinn city dir GUILD widow
- . 1873 city dir
- . 1880 Census LUCAS John B HOH
- . 1881 Oct 13 Did Mortgage to LEIGHTON
- . 1884 Note by Lee (TAYLOR) Middleton
- . 1900 Census LUCAS John B HOH
- . 1903 Cutter St incident
- . 1905 Cutter St resident
- . 1907 SMITH, Mary I death +

Above are examples of level 6 folders. They are content
folders within a person's folder. The '.' will be explained
later.

To put the folder levels into a closer context, here is the
ladder:

Level 1- Genealogy ALL HERE >

Level 2a -Family Research - PEOPLE (and 2b- Genealogy
Overflow) >

Level 3- 1st Initial = A-Z birth names >

Level 4- Surname birth names >

Level 5- PEOPLE in appropriate surname folder (SMITH Mary file is here) >

Level 6- Contents for each person (the content folders for SMITH Mary are here).

Following the above will surprise you with how easy it will be to find who you want and what you want.

NOTE: IF you have chosen to scan your paper files (manila folders) to the computer people files prior to organizing the information already held in your computer, do the computer organization now. Take it slow to make sure you do not do duplicate people folders on a person.

*

Chapter 4 - What Genealogy Program and Some Tips

There are a lot of varied genealogy programs on the market. Each promotes themselves as the best, of course. I have researched them all and tried most.

Some people actually use two or more genealogy programs due to what one may do and the other will not do. Some people try to keep each totally current with the use of GEDCOMs, an outdated item. The problem with GEDCOMs is that it only transfers certain information and far from all that can be entered into a program. For safety sake, currently think of a GEDCOM as name, birth, death, and the marriage date only. The history of GEDCOM can be found on the web if you are not familiar with the term or what it is.

Some programs offer more space than others for the entry of information. Some programs offer a few bells and whistles others do not. I've never heard anyone say they like their program 100%. The key is to pick one that allows you to do as much as possible and then YOU choose what you want to use with the program.

To compare or pick a genealogy program, there are comparison charts on the web but knowing when those sites are updated is important as programs are changing. Research each in depth as you do not want to change to a different program after entering hundreds or thousands of people into the one you first use. The thought of rechecking all those files on some type of a transfer between programs is daunting.

To start, at this point with your 'ORGANIZATION', with whatever program you are using, only enter the names, births, marriages, and deaths. It is a good idea to get into the habit of entering a person into your genealogy program right after you get the 'People Folder' made in your computer files. Make sure you DO enter the people under the correct parents if the parents are known.

Right now what you are concerned with is organizing and you will be building files IN your genealogy program, not entering details other than the identifiers (name, birth, death, marriage). Again, make sure you have a person under the right parents, if known.

Do not get side tracked. Further in this book there is more concerning entering further information that can be found on a document.

I am an avid TMG user and I cannot at this time make a recommendation for another program. My program works even though it is off of the market and until things settle in the future with other makers, I'll keep using it. Currently there is nothing that can take the transfer off all the information I have entered into it.

*

Chapter 5 – Old emails with family information

Did you know you can save old emails in other places than your email program?

Did you know that emails are a SOURCE for information you receive that you did not know or can be considered a SOURCE for confirming what you had found or been told elsewhere?

For safety sake, and for keeping track of everything someone sent to you or you sent to them that you saved, I will first begin this explanation with a labeling format.

The below is actually very simple but I am putting detailed instructions for this as few know how to do any part of this.

To explain first your new labels you will give to an email: How to label those old emails to make sense is a simple date and name process. You will be storing them elsewhere than in your email program and you will keep your email program 'clean' from older emails, ones you may have to hunt and peck for IF you remember they are there.

As you do this and you find those old emails it is important to understand that the date you receive an email is important. To rename it for filing, as you 'refile' it, look first at the date. Let's say you received and sent total of six emails in one day, they being to and from one person. Using this formula, they will file themselves in order. You just have to set where to file them.

Take the date of 'Sat/9/2/2006 5:51 AM' as an example. You will file this as '2006 09 02 0551am' (with no quotes) and add name information such as (example) CARVER to SMITH. That makes your filing label in full as '2006 09 02 0551am CARVER to SMITH'. If the time was pm, just change the 'am' to 'pm'. Note where I have added extra zero's for dates and early times.

You will be saving the emails to TWO folders in your main genealogy computer folder. One is to keep all emails from and to one person in one file. The second is to keep information ABOUT a person in the correct people folders.

Email Save #1 (the first file for saving email contact letters): The first folder to save your old emails to should be in a folder named 'Genealogy CONTACTS – Family Connections' (no quotes).

It is in layer #2 of your folders, a 3rd sub-folder at level #2. This folder will keep everything from and to each person and all people you have been in contact with grouped in one area.

- Family Research - PEOPLE
- Genealogy CONTACTS - Family Connections
- Genealogy Overflow

Above is an example of level #2, adding 'Genealogy CONTACTS – Family Connections'.

You now want to make a sub-folder IN 'Genealogy CONTACTS -Family Connections' labeled by the contact persons last name and then first name. This is a layer #3, but level #1 within the contacts folder.

At times you may receive emails from someone who does not want to give you their last name. It does rarely happen. Examples for folder headings are shown below. Note that it is important to identify what these folders are in each heading as it is easy to search into a wrong area to possibly a person in your People folders (research folders) by the same name.

- email Beth yuib@erinet.com (SMITH line)
- email CARVER Joan
- email JONES Mary
- email MOORE Beth
- email TAYLOR Ralph

Above, shows level #3 being placed under 'Genealogy CONTACTS – Family Connections'. This is the second level of 'Genealogy CONTACTS – Family Connections'.

To Clarify: (1) Open your main genealogy folder. (2) Make your Genealogy Contacts – Family Contacts folder. (3) Make a sub-folder in that new CONTACT folder titled 'email xxxnamexxx' for each person you have been in contact with (not for each email) as shown above for level #3.

Note that it is really hard to add a family name line of research following the label name, as shown for 'Beth' above in the example, as often an email may be about varied family surnames considering the women.

Doing the above for the emails you want to keep will now keep all emails FROM or TO a person in one file for each person on the other end of your emails. You may want to keep emails for people that were not connected to you as a reference that you have been in contact with that person as it stops repetitive contacting by you and references if they contact you again.

Email Save #2 (the second file to save to for email contacts and letters): The second folder to save emails to is the PEOPLE file that the email is about, or rather who the information pertains to. This is NOT the person the email is from or to. It is who is being talked about. This is the 'Family Research – PEOPLE' folder files.

Of course one email can contain information on more than one person so you can actually save a copy of the first 'save #1' to each person mentioned. This also helps you build your people files in the folder named 'Family Research – PEOPLE'. If you do not have a People file or folder in your computer already made for a person mentioned within an email, make one now.

How to save and file an email into (1) the Contact folder and (2) the PEOPLE FOLDER file:

(1) Go to the original email in your email program and open it.

(2) Click on 'Forward' as if you were going to forward it to someone else.

(3) You will see a small area above the text IN the email. You CAN add notes into this at this time (or at a later time,

then doing another 'save' with no name or subject change) if needed – like 'the person had the wrong family line', 'email dead with date' or 'this person has died' or whatever details you may want to add.

(4) Click on 'File'.

(5) Click on 'Save As'.

(6) Scroll to your main genealogy folder ('Genealogy ALL HERE').

(7) Click on 'Genealogy Contacts' (one of the folders you made at level 2).

(8) Open the contact person name folder (that should have been made prior to doing the save – see level #3 this chapter above). This is the person at the other end of the email.

(9) Type in your new 'File Name' (see examples at end of this chapter) IN the 'SUBJECT' line and DO leave (or re-add) the 'msg' showing at the end as you save it. Then save it.

(10) Close the 'forward' email. (This closed 'forward' may show in your draft or deleted folder. If so, once you are sure it is saved, that extra copy should be deleted.)

(11) Go to the persons email contact folder and make sure the email is there. If you missed a layer, drag it to the correct person in the email Contact folder. Sometimes opening a second window helps with dragging items.

(12) You can now delete out the original email in your email program or if you want, save it (drag it) to a new folder in

your email program named to show you have copied it (Emails Family COPIED) with subfolders per contact name.

To SAVE it to WHO the email is about (Save #2) being one or more people, go to the first save (the one you just did) in the contact folder and do a 'copy'. Then go to your people folders and 'paste' it to each person.

Make sure adjustments were done in your new headings (your newly saved email copies) with the names to show who it was to and who it was from. Continue with your next email.

I myself delete emails out of my email program after I do the above two saves. I found not doing so just builds confusing clutter that is not needed. After a few of these saves, you'll be a professional at it. This is your choice. If you are unsure of what you are doing at this time, save it to a newly named email folder in your email program named to show you have copied contents within it.

Remember that something someone tells you that you did not know is now your documentation, otherwise now known as your source or a source. It may be an old family story that you will not find in any official government record or book. If it came to you in an email, you now have saved that documentation in a findable location. Remember too that the person on the other end of that email should ALSO have a People folder made if it IS a family member and should be entered into your genealogy program.

Following is examples of a few emails shown in a Contact folder named 'email JONES Mary'. These were set into their own individual folder as a Word Document was made for each with my own notes added for each email. You do NOT have to do single folders for emails to and from a single person if nothing is added to accompany the email. They will line up as shown below but without the folders showing as you will have just the emails.

2004 03 14 0631am JONES to SMITH

2004 03 14 1100am SMITH to JONES

2007 11 01 0401am JONES to SMITH

2007 11 03 1224pm SMITH to JONES

By glancing at the above it tells you that JONES made the first contact and Smith wrote the last email. It also lines up all emails in the correct date format, oldest to newest in this view.

*

Chapter 6 - Census and Other Visuals

If you would like to add a copy of the original census page or pages to a summary there is an easy way to do it without showing the entire census page. You can show the heading and the family members only.

Download a free 'snipping' or 'snap' program if you do not have one. They seriously only take a few minutes to learn.

With using this tool you can snap views, including doing a crop and save, saving it as a JPG. You can then add JPG's to a word document using the Word insert feature. If you need to do two 'snaps', as with the following census view' and want them to show as one view as with the census view below, do a snap of each area and paste each into a Word Document. The saved size will depend on how large you made your screen for doing the snaps. After both are on your Word document, then copy that as one view with the snap program and save it as a JPG/JPEG. You can always size the JPG down if needed.

Once that is done, you can then attach it to your final summary, attach it to an email or where you need to use it. Once saved to one person listed, you can always copy and paste that to other people folders that may be listed on the document.

You can adjust the size in two ways. First would be by the size of the copy you do (enlarge or shrink the view prior to your snip) and the other is adjusting the size once it is in your word document using the size feature after you attach (copy & paste or insert) it.

A finished view follows that uses two saves, this being from the 1880 census and it was saved to each person shown. You can use the copy tool for adding a part of any item.

Note that with a census, you can actually have three or four needed views with the previous or next page and some census's had extra information for some people.

Following is a crop from an 1861 map using the tool. This was actually saved to nine different people.

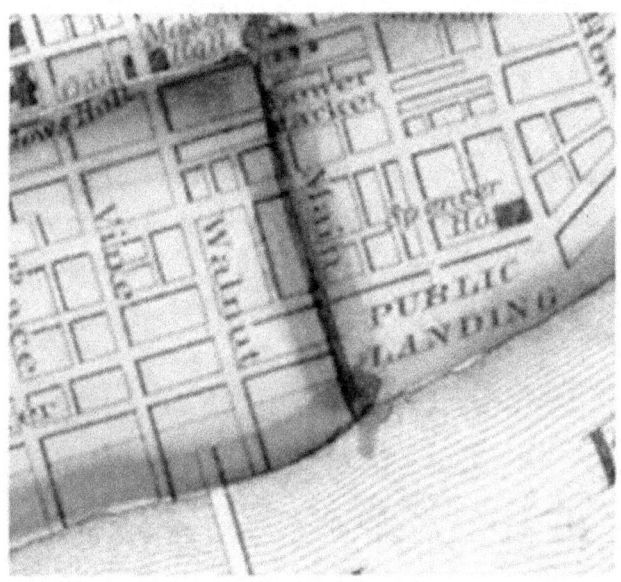

The snipping tool comes in handy for a lot of uses when you really need to copy something from one item. Get the view you want and save in a JPG format. It is great for copying and showing old document signatures. You can also enlarge things like this first. Enlarge from your saved scan or JPG, crop to what you want to snip, then snip, and then save it.

When you save something with a snipping tool, you do want to save it to the person folder it concerns naming it to identify exactly what it is. An example would be the city name, the year, the part of the city. The preceding shown signatures were actually saved to three files, the subject who was the son, the step-father and the mother. One was a save and the other two were a copy and paste.

Three free programs to snap views are

http://www.capture-screenshot.org/snipping-tool/

http://www.mirekw.com/winfreeware/mwsnap.html

http://www.techradar.com/downloads/snipping-tool-plus

*

Chapter 7 - Photographs

Do you have photographs that are loose or ones in a variety of albums that you would like to reorganize? Are you in a situation where varied family members all want some or all of the old family photos from childhood and those that exist from earlier time frames? Why not share all with everyone, that including ones the family members have in their possession? You can do so by scanning them.

This is a project to work on after all of your paper and computer treasures are organized and you have your people files made. Of course, new people files are always going to happen and some new people files may be made due to the photographs you have. Do not forget to add a new person to your genealogy program if they are not added there!

First organize the loose photographs by people name and year or assumed year. This helps you match in photos for time periods and even for ones taken on a same day.

While you are working thru your sorting and before you actually start scanning, decide what format you want to save your scans as. When you scan a photograph, you can 'save as' in a variety of formats. Four choices are JPG, TIF, PNG, and GIF. Read up on those. JPG also known as JPEG is not the best quality but many do not want to take up larger computer space with saving things and the quality difference is not noticed by the novice. When scanning, you DO, especially for a JPG, want a high resolution. You do not want excessive but more resolution than what automatically may come up by the program. Your scanner program may tell you that the higher resolution is not needed, but it is wise to ignore that as you want an excellent copy of the original. Should you decide you want the very best quality and are willing to use up the computer drive space, I have read that you should choose a TIF format. I myself use the JPG option and I scan at a higher resolution than my scanner wants to use. As a test for size differences, scan a photo and save it in all formats. Then check the sizes of each under properties and also visually check for differences. You also may want to print each version to see what the different versions look like in print.

DO – DO – DO OVER scan past the edges of an original photograph. You will use the crop feature in your scanning program for this. Do not forget the backs if ANY information is shown there. Scanning past the edges can often be a great aid with dating a photo and it then also gives you a true reproduction of the original photograph.

FILING your scanned photographs:

Assuming you have no photographs in your computer, start a folder that says 'PHOTOGRAPHS – FAMILY' or any name that works for you. To start, put it on your desktop for ease in finding it when placing photos. If your program wants to open to your My Documents folder after scanning, you can place it there. Some programs or computers will change to the main folder area no matter where it is after a few scans if that is where you are always heading to, so test that out.

Within your 'PHOTOGRAPHS – FAMILY' folder you will be placing many sub-folders, one for each photo or if many are on one day, it will hold them in that one folder.

NAMING your folder: The ideal option is to start with the year or year 'ca' (1900 or 1900 ca), the last name, first name & event in a word or three. Do the best you can but shoot for a year first if at all possible.

An option that I like to use is making the first word 'Photo' as it helps me know what is in that folder in the person folder. It also helps me in various other ways too. You do not need to use capital letters for the word as shown below.

- PHOTO 1880 ca SMITH Mary - Cincinnati OH
- PHOTO 1900 SMITH Mary - Anniversary Photo
- PHOTO 1905 SMITH Mary - with children

NAMING your photograph: Naming your photograph is usually the same as naming your folder except for adding a little bit of information. Added information would be x100% as original, x400%, face crop x800%, color, b&w, and further as needed. Your computer will add the ending .jpg or whatever your type of scan is saved as so do NOT add that on your own. Examples:

1880 SMITH John Indpls x100% color.jpg

1880 ca SMITH John face crop x800% color.jpg

1880 ca SMITH John face crop x800% b&w.tif

1880 SMITH John waist up crop x300% color.gif

With one photo you can actually end up with many views when you realize how you can bring out detail with cropping to an area of the photo. One example: I have a photo from the very early 1900s of a great grandfather working in front of a tent that has a white spot on it. I scanned that area (crop) at a VERY large size and resolution. It turned out he had a bathtub medallion on the tent. This told me that the magic elixir he made and sold was to put into a bathtub and people were able to bathe at the place (maybe a fair) where he was selling it at that day. What it did not tell me is if he was able to furnish hot water at the tent. If nothing else, it was part of his sales gimmick. Then doing scans on two other people shown with him (crops) at the higher settings, I was able to identify who two other people were from matching other photos to them. This was later verified as the correct people by a long lost family member.

Decide if you want to label your photograph scans by the year first or by surname first. Naming a photo can be (examples):

Example #1: 1897 SMITH John at Cincinnati homestead

Example #2: SMITH John 1897 Cincinnati homestead

If you have a few photos taken on the same day, you may have to add an 'a', 'b', or 'c' format or 1, 2, 3 just prior to the '.' (dot).   Example: SMITH John 1897 Cincinnati Homestead 1.jpg. If you have ten or more photographs taken on that same day, change the 1 to 01 and so on thru number 9.

You may decide you want the year of birth and death to show with the photo label. In that case, use this format (shown for use for more than one view of the same year and place photo with adding the 1):

1897 SMITH John 1850-1907 at Cincinnati Homestead 1.jpg

For an assumed year, and if your label choice is to list the year first, an assumed year would be entered as '1901 ca'. Example:

1897 ca SMITH John 1850-1907 Cincinnati Homestead 1.jpg

If you are labeling by name first, your 'ca' would show as:

SMITH John 1850-1907 ca 1897 Cincinnati Homestead 1.jpg

Scanning Options:

You may want to scan in varied sizes. FIRST always scan at 100% (full size) and scan the back if anything is on it. This opens the door to doing a folder within that new main photograph folder to keep all together.

Always scan in color and also do so in black and white if the original is black and white. You can print a color photo in black and white per printer options BUT you do want an exact duplication. Notes of what you have done can be typed up in a Word Document and saved with the photo in that photo file with the photograph.

On the original first scan, ALWAYS crop to the outer edge so you DO show the entire photo. Sometimes the edge can actually help date a photo.

Following are three visuals of what you can do for one photo showing the front and the back. The first two are scanned x 100%. The third is a crop scanned x 800%. Tight crop visuals were done for all four children x 800% but only one is shown here. The front was also scanned a second time x 500%. These are the black and white views of the color (sepia tone) photos showing the aging of the photo, dirt and all.

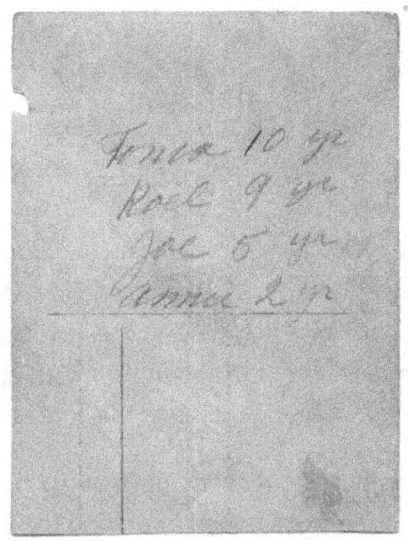

Following is an option that can be done that few think about. Have you ever seen a very old photo that has been ruined by hand writing on the original? It is nice they saved the information but …..! You can add words to your scan but NOT ON the photo.

Over scan it a lot at the bottom. Save it. Go back to that 'save' and add words into that open area you just made and resave with adding 'words' to that second save label. You will then have two views, one being an oversized blank word area if needed. You will possibly need to do a crop and re-save to remove excess space not used by words. You can add anything you want to within the word area, even the date scanned, scanned by who, and the settings you used.

 To print something like that you have two choices. Print with the words you have added or crop to the photo and print the photo only. As long as you DO NOT resave that crop you have just done, you will not alter the original. You can save that crop adding 'crop no words' to the label for it. A added benefit to saving your scan with blank space is that in the future you can change the wording. Rename it before saving to keep your blank copy.

IF a photo is large enough, you can just print it with the words and it will print on two papers. Put the word paper on the back side and put it into a front-back clear frame or dual frame.

A free program to add words is found at http://www.faststone.org/ and it offers many other features for use. (I have no connection to this company.) REMEMBER when you add words, add the word 'words' to the photo labeled version so you do not alter your original blank word photograph.

Following are two examples of over scanning (scanning way over the edge) to add words, with the words added. The first is one of those tiny dime store machine photos. This actually has her finger prints on it and it is noted with the photo in the wording. The second is of a color slide that was scanned which is shown here in black and white. They are shown here in a much smaller scale than possible and too small for you to read the print.

Anne Christine FLINT
Age 16. 1936
A dime store machine photo cut from the strip and sent to brother, Bill FLINT.
- Enlargement -
Two beige areas are her fingerprints as taken from machine wet.

1959 December

Our dog Puggy and her pups that survived.
The pups were way to large for her and it took a vet for their birth.
The first born died at home. Then she went to the vets.

We called one Brownie and another Blackie.
The pups went to other homes when old enough.

937 Larriwood Dr., Kettering, Ohio 45429

Slide developed: Dec 1959.
Scan of slide Aug 2006 ~ Full photo shown. No color enhancements or adjustments.
Photo taken by LeRoy ST. FELIX.
Carey ST. FELIX has the original.

Following is an example of a photo 'blank' follows. Under that is a crop from the full photograph with no word space. After words are added to a blank, re-crop out excess and save with the description to reflect it has words.

NOTE: The blank area where words can go above is white.

The following is a crop view from the above. You can see that with cropping and enlarging a lot of detail is shown that does not show in the original.

Cropping to print does not affect the original with the words UNLESS you save the new crop OVER the current photo name (you did not change the name) should you have decided to save that crop. Be sure to change a name when doing a crop of the original. Adding 'crop' or even '2' at the end prior to the .jpg word will work.

Not many people realize that they can also add information to the properties section of a photo after it is scanned. Right click on your view after you have saved it. Go to 'Properties'. Click on 'Details'. Scroll down to 'Comments'.

A box will open where you can add a lot of information about the photo. You should be able to see 'Date taken' which is the date you scanned the photo and your name or computer name should automatically be showing too. This information cannot be seen by just viewing a photo and definitely not be seen in a printed photo from that scan. The 'date' shown there may change however when you make changes to the properties.

When you scan a photograph, you can 'save as' in a variety of formats. Four choices are JPG, TIF, PNG, and GIF. Read up on those. JPG also known as JPEG is not the best quality but many do not want to take up larger computer space with saving things and the quality difference is not noticed by the novice.

If you want an index list of photos that you have scanned, you can actually set the 'View' of that new folder to List or a Size of icons. That is a visual index and you can sort per your choice. Do not waste time trying to do a separate list. When you open a folder, any folder anywhere, in case you do not know, can be viewed per your settings. Look above to the word 'View'. Left click. Choose how you want to view those contents. 'Details' will list as a summary.

There are programs that say they can organize your photos for you. What happens if that program does not work with future computers? What happens if you give a copy of your photos to someone and they cannot find anything as they do not have that program? Think ahead and do your labels to make sense to someone 200 years from now.

YOUR SECOND PHOTO SAVE:

 As you scan and you are complete with that photo or group of photos in one folder, you want to do a copy and paste of the FOLDER and place a copy in the individual person people folders for that person or people (copy and paste). IF there is more than one person in a photo, do a paste to all individual person folders pertaining to the photo. You will then have the photos in a main photo file showing ALL photographs and a second copy with the person it goes to. Over time, as projects come up, you will be very glad you did this and it is a quick thing to do.

You can do a third save, that being to a folder for just the older photos, all copied to that folder also. This may be handy if you know at times you will mail the views to other people in bulk.

Tips on storing original photos:

After scanning a photo, here is a safe and easy way to store the originals and it includes protection against scratches.

For your original photographs you will need the following items unless you want to deal with many photograph albums.

1: Cardboard photo boxes or cardboard file index card boxes. Strive for Archival Quality. For larger photos, you want archival quality boxes. Large items of any nature, even old Bibles, should be stored in archival boxes.

2: Plastic sleeves, like fitted plastic bags, the type that baseball cards are set into &/or hard plastic sleeves, also used for baseball cards, all of a size to fit the photo loosely. They come in a variety of sizes and can usually be ordered thru a baseball or hobby shop and also on the web. Make sure what you get is archival quality.

3: Yellow sticky papers.

4: An archival pen. You will not be writing on any original photos but you want something safe for being near a photo.

Write details about the photo on the BACK side of the sticky paper and attach it into the sleeve. Then add your photo putting the back side of the photo towards the sticky.

To file them into the boxes, it is your choice per how you decide to file them. You can do so by year or name. Large tabbed index file cards can also be used to separate years or names.

MORE on how to save information with photographs, along with more samples, can be found in my book titled *Photographs How to Keep the Details and Story with Any Photo In a Permanent Way without Altering the Original Photograph*.

*

Chapter 8 – Summaries: How To and Why

You should now have your paper files organized and scanned to your individual people folders in your computer. All of the computer genealogy items that you had in your computer should now be organized and into those same individual people files also. You may have your photographs done or are doing that later.

Do not be surprised if you later find a random loose thing somewhere at home or in the computer as that does happen. Just follow the organization plan.

.....

Pick a person to work on to do your first summary. Enter this person into your genealogy program NOW if you have not done so prior. Do the Name, Birth Date, Marriage and Death Date if known. You can add more details for the person if you know your program but other items can be added later. Entering the above at least is organizing and you can work off of your summary later for further information entry if you choose to do so.

.....

A summary is just what it says, a summary of persons life. These are done with Word Document or an equivalent program (see tools) with a computer. This is an item you want to do for a variety of reasons.

Do not worry about doing summaries for everyone all at once. You will work on these as you want to work on your choice of person. As you work on your summary it is a perfect time to add further details about the person into your genealogy program.

.....

Each person gets their own summary. You will be looking at everything you have in that persons computer file. As you work on this DO expect to be doing more research for other people as you work on their summary. You may find that as you are organizing one person's folders that there are things needed and you may be surfing the web for days for things on just that one person.

Keep in mind that documents for another person may refer to this person also. You can easily go to another person's folder, copy the item and paste it to the folder (the person) you are working on. This is where with organizing that the copy and paste comes in to varied folders if multi people are mentioned on an item.

Begin with who you want to. You can begin with yourself if you want. I recommend starting with someone you have very little information on for learning purposes and you can always add to a summary later.

....

On my main screen using Word Document, I have one Word Document saved that is labeled '! Summary blank' (no quotes). You can also place this within the main Genealogy folder.

Following is the blank summary you will make in Word document. This is where you are going to enter information about a person. Open your word program and type in the following, then SAVE IT as 'Blank Summary'. Not showing in this view is Birth and further date items as I enter those below and add sentences. All is lined up by DATES like a timeline. You can add the birth year and death year after the name that will be on the line after the heading of '! Summary'.

! Summary

Name variations:

...

Father:

Mother:

Siblings:

Spouse:

Children:

SS #:

...

Tribal Pages link:

Blog overflow:

When you start a summary for a person, open this 'Summary BLANK'.

Next to the word 'Summary' on the 'form' you will add the last name, first name birth year and death year. Example: SMITH John 1850-1925.

Save it to the People folder you are working on and change the label (the document label) in that save (Example: ! Summary SMITH John 1850-1925).

Close the original 'blank' word document that you first opened. You do not need to resave it. The blank you just closed will be there for your next person in the 'Summary Blank' folder.

Go to the persons file where you just saved that summary with basic information. Rename that summary document if need be as some computers will not save the '!' or the '-'. 'Rename' the summary to reflect the full title. You will have to rename it adding the '!' as it will not stay in the first save and any dashes will have to be retyped. The '!' use is to keep it at the top of any other word documents that may be added to the file. An example of a finished summary title should show as (example): '! Summary SMITH Elizabeth 1899- 1950' without the quotes.

After filling in those lines shown in the blank summary, save it again and continue adding information for the person now or later, adding in your findings. I chose to do list events by date. That makes my summaries time lines with facts and visuals added but you can do it as you prefer. A somewhat older example of how I start out with the 'blank' is shown below. You can see the entire large final work at the web address shown. (Note: I have that webpage so packed, that at times words appear tiny in areas.)

WORKING COPY updated Sep 2, 2012 (Mark in RED areas to follow up on.)

Uploaded to the blog: http://stfelixmdflint.blogspot.com/2013/02/amons-john-julius-1855-1907.html

Entered into TribalPages: TO DO

John Julius AMONS [JR]

Father: John J. AMONS [SR], born ca 1833 born Pennsylvania.

Mother: Mary Inez (SMITH) AMONS – GUILD – LUCAS born 24 Jul 1834 Pleasant Ridge, Hamilton Co., Ohio.

Siblings: Yes.

Spouse: Carrie Eudora BLACK, born 04 Feb 1856 Hamilton Co., Ohio.

Children: Birdie Estella AMONS, born 27 Aug 1887, California, Hamilton Co., Ohio.

Johns adult description: Grey eyes, black hair, has a dark complexion, and is 5 feet 7 inches tall.

1855 March 18 – Birth: Conflicting dates have been found for the birth date for John J. AMONS. Per information in the large interment book at Wesleyan Cemetery he was born on 18 March 1855, his parents being John J. AMONS [SR] and Mary Inez SMITH.

You can add as much detail as you want to a summary. This is YOUR summary work. Strive to make the summaries complete with all you can find for a person.

To add things to the summary and organize a person's file: Look at what you are holding in this persons folder. Start with one item. Enter it into your summary. DO enter all details for the item. When you are done with that item, do a folder for it within that person's folder if there is not one for that item (like a birth certificate). Begin with a dot (if you are done with the item), space, date of item (year for), last name, first name and what it is. (Samples follow.)

As you add in the information to your summary from what you have in your computer for that person, do a folder for each item as shown below. After you DO have everything possible for that item entered into your summary, rename the item folder by putting a dot in front of that folder name. Example: You have a folder named SMITH John 1875-1951. Within that folder you have subfolders by various names. One named '1895 Military SMITH John 1875-1951' now has all information and visuals entered into your summary. Change the subfolder name to '. 1965 Military SMITH John 1875-1951'. This tells you that you are done with that folder and it will cycle to the top of the list depending on your sort setting. Continue with all 'item' folders for that person.

When you are finished with item folders, rename the PERSON'S folder with the dot and it will cycle to the top. This tells you that you are done with that person concerning information entry with what you have. That persons main folder that holds the subfolders will now be named (example) '. SMITH John 1875-1951'. IF you are sure you can still find more for that person, do NOT rename the person's main folder with that 'dot'.

An example of a person's folder where all CONTENTS have been added to the summary follows:

- . 1909 Birth Marcella
- . 1909 city dir Marcella
- . 1910 census HOH FELIX HENRY C
- . 1910 city dir Marcella
- . 1911 city dir & map Daniel St Dayton 1901 map
- . 1911 city dir Marcella
- . 1911 death cert ST FELIX Marcella
- . 1911 ST FELIX, Marcella Woodlawn Cemetery
- . Photo Marcella Gails wall
- ! Summary ST FELIX Marcella 1909-1911.docx

An example of a person's main folder for one person that is DONE and nothing can be added shows the dot or period at the front of the line.

- . ST FELIX Marcella 1909-1911 dau to Harry C & QUINN

The above summary with visuals can be seen at http://stfelixmdflint.blogspot.com/2012/12/st-felix-marcella-1909-1911.html. Items were housed in her folder. The summary that was done for her was copied to the website.

Note: 'Done' does not mean that you cannot add more if more if more is found for a person.

You have been organizing an individual person's folder contents. Remember that dot at the beginning of a person's folder tells you that person is done. HOWEVER, it is not done until you have entered that person you're your genealogy program.

Later you can add more to your genealogy program if wanted. Just build YOUR routine.

 If your summary is totally done, as done as you are willing to work on that person, see if your program allows you to attach your summary to that person IN the program or if you can copy it to a 'tag'. It will save you a lot of work.

*

Chapter 9 - Down the Road and Optional

Following is down the road, long after you have organized all of your paper, computer and photograph items. Do not let this confuse you now. It is an option for you to keep others updated with what you are doing. It can also 'catch' unknown family with their web searches if put on a blog or website.

.....

Using tags in your genealogy program that you can design or name allows you to know what you have done!

.....

A 'TAG' and what that means. To easily explain it I will so by an example. You have a person who has a name. The name is a 'tag'. The person has a birthdate and that is a 'tag'. The person has a child and that is a 'tag'. Anything you enter for a person is considered a tag. Some genealogy programs may refer to another word for 'tag'.

If your genealogy program allows you to make a tag (the TMG program does) you want to go to one 'tag' named Note. Duplicate it. Then rename the duplication to '! Summary' without the quote marks.

You will eventually attach or copy and paste your summary to that tag named '! Summary'. The reason for the '!' is so that it is found on top area of the tags used for an individual people without searching for it. That makes adding summaries for a person a lot simpler and at instant glance you can see what you have done by looking at that person's tags used.

I do not recommend adding a summary to a person in the program until you have finished researching the person. If you do attach it, you can replace it. The advantage of this attachment is that the tag shown for a person in the program tells you that you have researched all you can for the person. For a few of my people I actually have a Word Document listing what I would like to find, but the searches have been useless.

Below is from a page I have in my program for a long ago family member and the tags shown are for just what I have found for him. This shows three tags I have made for him on top, all beginning with '!' and I will explain.

! Tribal pages link
! Blog uploaded
! Summary
Name-Var
Birth
Emigration
Immigratn
Marriage
Son-Bio
Natlzation
Dau-Bio
SSN
Residence
Residence
Death

Following explains part of what is shown.

(1) ! Tribal pages link (this is a tag): I had been entering things also into free (or paid for more bells and whistles) site on line for family to check what I am doing. (Currently I am redoing that for my family members.) You can later do that by use of a GEDCOM which is limited with what it transfers.

- Family has the web link and it saves me from doing a lot of emails.

- This allows them to let me know what I may be missing and also allows the elderly instant access to see it all.

-     When I have entered a person to TribalPages (www.TribalPages.com), I note that direct link for that person as a tag in my TMG program. I enter the link to the TribalPages website page in the memo that will show when I open the tag in my program. This link also shows on #2 below.

(2) ! Blog uploaded (this is a tag): For some people I have an excess of information and a lot of photos that will not fit into the free version of TribalPages noted above. For a few I have very old original passports too. The full summary and all else, that including the passport pages in JPEG format, are uploaded to a blog.

At the blog I reference the page as an overflow to the TribalPages page showing that link. At the TribalPages link I also reference the direct blog to the person showing that link there too. It is a circle to information, if you will. My choice for a blog is www.blogspot.com for which at the side bar I have added an index, people reached by link at the blog.

(3) ! Summary (this is a tag): As mentioned above, I have attached my summary to the person in my genealogy program.

This is not quick work but it works for many depending on their needs.

*

Chapter 10 - Sources - Oh My!

Sources are a somewhat confusing thing to work with. There are books written just for explaining them.

Basically a source tells you where you got your information from; the what, the where and so on.

If you are familiar with web searches, you most likely have seen sources quoted when you find information. A site like www.familysearch.org will show their source at the bottom of page.

So what do you list as your source? You got it from a website, right? Well yes, but should you list their source? Actually yes that too.

However, if you do not want to deal with sources at this time as you are expected to do; you are not yet ready to deal with entering sources into a genealogy program, you can at least save the web link but they can change.

Here are two options:

In an individual persons computer folder, for each item you have for that person (separate folder for each item), you can add a word document for that item and name it (example) '1889 Birth notes Jones Sue'.

Within that 'note' you can list the link you found the item at. At least you can easily get back to it on the web. You can also copy the source information shown there for that item. If it came from a paid membership site it is a good idea to copy that source information while you are there.

SO, for full reference, you have a live link and their reference (example) showing:
https://familysearch.org/pal:/MM9.1.1/V9S4-NZQ

and

"United States Social Security Death Index," index, FamilySearch (https://familysearch.org/pal:/MM9.1.1/V9S4-NZQ : accessed 09 Jul 2014), Harry Felix, Dec 1975; citing U.S. Social Security Administration, Death Master File, database (Alexandria, Virginia: National Technical Information Service, ongoing).

You can enter that into your genealogy program when you are ready to deal with sources. You can also add it to your summary. Word Documents do allow the use of Endnotes and Footnotes.

If you need to read up on sources, it is said your best read on it is titled Evidence by Mills.

Very often you will find on the web works done by others. Use that information as leads ONLY, not absolute truth. There is overwhelming errors put out by others, often done by assumptions and not in depth research for proof. They website you found that 'something' at would be a source. If you can make contact with a person for it, be sure to do good documentation with what they furnish to you and list them in your contact list.

I found it is very helpful to also use a snipping tool to get visuals of things on line should the contact be by some type of message system on a website. I copy and paste the conversation to a Word Document. You can keep a copy in the Contact folder and also with the person the conversation is about.

*

Closing Note

I tried to keep the explanations easy to read and understandable along with being very specific on the previous pages. There is nothing worse for me than to read and read on useless pages just to be overwhelmed with glassy eyes.

I do want to mention that you can adjust your routine as it works for you. It is very important to get all steps in and the previous routine works best to avoid missing steps with saving items, information and documenting.

It is very important to have IN each person's folder everything you have for that person and achieving that is where you MUST be organized.

I have many computer people folders where people have dozens of items sitting there waiting for me to organize the contents. Knowing which is not complete is easy with that '.' (dot) in front of their name on their folder for the finished ones.

Your goal for the computer People Folders is:

(1) All you physically hold, including photographs, is scanned and a copy is in the persons file along with all things found on the web for that person.

(2) Each item is entered into a summary and into a genealogy program.

Taking on the project of family research IS a slow process, but you knew that didn't you.   Think of it as mental stimulation (exercise) and make good notes as you think of things you want or need to do!

Thank you and I sincerely hope this book helps you. Just remember it takes time to get organized and a good routine is needed for how you store and do things.

*

A note from the author:

When working with old records and reports, it becomes a challenge at times, especially when items are full of dust, mold and at times, other strange things like mouse droppings. I do strive for the best feedback possible.

If you enjoyed your experience with this book, your favorable feedback to where you purchased the book is very much appreciated.

Current books by KALTEN

and

News on upcoming books can be found at

http://BooksByKalten.blogspot.com/